INTRODUCTION

With the state of the world currently, it is becoming harder and harder for the average middle-class family to thrive. Many have argued with that with the way things are right now, the middle-class does not even *exist* anymore - you are either in the upper-class where you are well off and relatively unbothered with the state of the world or you are in the lower-class, struggling to make ends meet. The middle-class is rapidly shrinking and it is not hard to see why - with rising costs of living, inflation and a general feeling of unease and insecurity, many people are finding it hard to keep up with the Joneses, let alone get ahead.

This idea of being able to "*get ahead*" financially has become a mere dream for most people. In the past, people could reasonably expect to make more money as they got older and progressed in their careers. But now, wage growth has stagnated while the cost of living has continued to increase. This means that people are effectively working harder and harder just to stay in the same place - not getting ahead, but simply treading water.

For many individuals, the only solution for them to stay afloat has been to pick up another job or work significantly more hours at their current job, but this comes at a significant cost to all other aspects of their life. See, when we're dependent upon exchanging our time for money, as we do in a job, all other aspects of our lives will suffer at the expense of our financial improvement. We are not spending as much time with our friends and family which can lead to burdened relationships. We are not spending as much time preparing our own meals and being active which leads to potential health issues. And possibly most importantly, we are not able to have time for leisure and relaxing which could be of **immeasurable detriment** to our mental health.

With all of that said, I hope that the solution to this problem is clear at this point - we need to establish a way to earn income without sacrificing our time.

Enter passive income.

Establishing successful streams of passive income is *unequivocally* the best way to achieve financial freedom. If we are able to establish a successful passive income stream, we are no longer at the mercy of directly having to exchange our time for money - instead, we invest our time initially and then reap the rewards (i.e. money) later. This gives us back our time and allows us to live our lives on our own terms, not at the beck and call of our jobs.

Now before we go any further, we must establish one thing right away: passive income is not easy income. It is not a "get rich quick" scheme either - **passive income is hard work -** arguably, even harder than working a job is initially. I mean if it were easy, no one would ever work a day in their life! But despite it being difficult, it is most certainly worth pursuing.

Our time is our most valuable asset. It is something that can never be renewed or given back to us. Because of that, establishing passive income streams that allow us to spend more of our time how we would like is of paramount importance.

When you were young, your parents told you to eat your vegetables so you could grow up big and strong, right? The same idea applies here - we need to put in the hard work upfront so that we can reap the rewards later. With that being said, let's get started on taking a dive into the world of passive income.

CHAPTER 1
WHAT IS PASSIVE INCOME?

Many people can have different ideas of what passive income truly is. For some, it is simply making money without having to put in any active effort. For others, it is a way to make money while still being able to enjoy life and not have to work long hours every day. This begs the question - what *really* is passive income?

At its core, passive income is creating a stream of revenue that does not require active work on your part. This can come in a variety of forms ranging from the age-old method of earning interest in a savings account, all the way up to multi-faceted businesses that will be discussed throughout this book. The key is that it is something that can be earned without having to put in a lot of effort on a regular basis.

With passive income, there is a heavy emphasis on the words *"active work"*. Passive income is not earning income without doing any work. Instead, it is about finding ways to continue to earn money even when you are not actively working.

. . .

Because of this concept, passive income is not for everyone. The majority of people are used to earning a stable income for a specific amount of "active work". For example, you go to work for forty hours a week and you earn a guaranteed paycheck for that work two weeks later. This is the traditional way that people have earned income for centuries and since many people are stuck in that way of thinking, they are not familiar with the concept of delayed gratification after doing work. Passive income streams take time and effort to be established and cannot be expected to bring in profit immediately. These types of income streams require you to put in effort upfront and then let the stream run on its own eventually.

There is another problem with the traditional system that we just discussed - it puts a limit on how much you can earn. If you want to make more money, you have to put in more hours at work. And there are only so many hours in a day. This is where passive income comes in. You are no longer bound by the limits of how much "active work" you can engage in. Instead, you focus on establishing streams of income that can work for you.

Through this book, you will learn to do just that. This book is going to serve as an introduction to some basic ways you can earn passive income. This is by no means a comprehensive guide to any one specific way to earning income - instead, this book aims to serve as a launch pad for your own imagination.

CHAPTER 2

AFFILIATE MARKETING

When looking at all the different ways to start generating passive income, affiliate marketing is a great option. With affiliate marketing, you promote products or services and earn a commission whenever someone makes a purchase through your link.

Affiliate marketing is especially powerful because it allows you to establish a revenue stream off of a product that you did not create yourself. Because of it, you can really limit the amount of time invested because there is a product that already exists and you simply need to promote it.

If you're interested in affiliate marketing, there are a few things you need to keep in mind. First, you'll need to find products or services to promote. There are a few different ways to do this. You can either join an affiliate network or work with companies directly.

. . .

Affiliate networks are middlemen between affiliates and merchants. They provide affiliates with access to a variety of products from different companies in exchange for a commission on sales. Joining an affiliate network is a good option if you want to have a lot of choices when it comes to the products you promote. However, there are also some downsides to working with affiliate networks. The biggest downside to this is that affiliate networks usually participate in some type of revenue sharing agreement as they do operate as a middleman. Because of this, you are usually not earning the maximum amount that a company has allotted for its affiliates.

To resolve this, you can also work with companies directly to market their products without finding them through a separate affiliate network. Many companies have affiliate programs that you can sign up for. This gives you access to their products or services and allows you to earn a commission on sales. Beyond that, while many companies may not have a specific affiliate program set up, you can also reach out to them directly to see if there is a specific deal that you could work out with them. Many medium-to-small sized brands are very receptive to this approach and the benefit to this approach is that you can usually become one of the only affiliates for a specific brand which heavily cuts down on any competition you may have.

Once you've found some products or services to promote that have an affiliate offer present, the next step is to start promoting them. There are a few different ways to do this but they all have one similarity - you need to get your offer in front of an audience that is interested in it. One popular way to share these links is by writing blog posts relevant to the offer and then including your affiliate links within the article. Now if written-word media is not your style, you can also create YouTube videos and provide your affiliate links there. Finally, one of the simplest ways to share your affiliate links would be on social media such as on Facebook pages or within different subreddits on Reddit.

No matter what method you choose, be sure to track your results so that you know what's working and what isn't. This will help you adjust your strategy as needed and ensure that you're generating the most passive income possible.

CHAPTER 3
VENDING MACHINE BUSINESS

The next idea to earn passive income is by establishing a vending machine business. Now this passive income method is a personal favorite of mine and it has personally been one of my most successful revenue streams. It is a business that can be started with very little money and can generate a full-time income.

Vending machines are everywhere these days. You can find them in gas stations, grocery stores, malls, and even some office buildings. And they're not just selling candy and snacks anymore. You can now find vending machines that sell everything from personal toiletries to electronics. This shows that the vending machine business is one that is consistently evolving and because of that, there is always room for new talent to come in and apply their own ideas to the industry.

Starting a vending machine business is a great way to earn passive income because it requires very little day-to-day active work on your part. Once you have your vending machines set up, the large portion of what you have left to do on an active basis is stocking them with product and collecting the money - a task that you may only have to do bi-weekly and that can be quite easily outsourced. Outside of that, there are occasional situations where there are malfunctions with vending machines but with how simple they are and how much information is so readily available surrounding them, repairing them is not as difficult as it sounds. And for those who are not as mechanically inclined, this is another task that can be easily outsourced to make this business as hands-off as possible for you.

Of course, there is some work involved in setting up your vending machine business. The most difficult part, and possibly the most important, is that you will need to find locations for where to place your vending machines. This can be a difficult feat for many as there is definitely a calculated art to finding the perfect vending machine location. Some factors to look into are the amount of foot traffic present, the type of clientele at a particular location, and the proximity of your machine to competitors (such as other vending machines or even convenience stores). Thankfully, this is yet another task that can be outsourced to companies that actually specialize in locating vending machine locations for businesses.

Once this difficult task has been completed, you can then move on to other tasks such as negotiating leases with the property owners, as well as purchasing or leasing the vending machines themselves. While this option does sound like there is a lot of work associated with getting it set up, it is important to remember that a lot of these tasks can be outsourced to companies that specialize in completing them quickly and efficiently. Beyond that, once your business is all set up, it will be relatively hands off for you.

If you're looking for a passive income opportunity that can generate a full-time income, then starting a vending machine business is a great option. With very little work on your part, you can earn money 24/7 from your vending machines. So, if you're looking for a way to make money while you sleep, then this is the perfect opportunity for you.

CHAPTER 4
CRYPTOCURRENCY STAKING

t's no surprise that over the past few years, cryptocurrency has seen a dramatic rise in popularity. While many people day-trade cryptocurrency as a revenue stream, this method much more active than passive. Since we are looking for passive income streams, cryptocurrency staking is a great way for us to be able to leverage the popularity of cryptocurrency in earning passive income.

Staking is the process of holding onto your cryptocurrency coins in order to help verify transactions on the blockchain and earn rewards for doing so. It's a relatively simple process and doesn't require much technical knowledge, making it a great way for beginners to get started in the world of cryptocurrency.

So how does staking work? When you stake your coins, you are essentially putting them up as collateral in order to help verify transactions on the blockchain. In return for helping to secure the network, you will earn rewards in the form of newly minted coins. The amount of rewards you earn will depend on the size of your stake and the length of time you keep your coins staked. You are able to look up the estimated reward before you stake your coins so that you can establish if you are making a worthwhile investment.

If you're interested in earning passive income through cryptocurrency staking, there are a few things you need to know before getting started. First, you'll need to choose a cryptocurrency that offers staking as a way to earn rewards. Not all cryptocurrencies offer this option, so be sure to do your research before selecting one. Once you've chosen a cryptocurrency, you'll need to acquire some coins and store them in a wallet that supports staking. Finally, you'll need to set up your wallet to begin receiving rewards.

While cryptocurrency staking can be a great way to earn passive income, it's important to remember that it comes with some risks. The value of your coins can fluctuate wildly, and you could end up losing money if the price of the cryptocurrency falls. Therefore, it's important to only invest what you can afford to lose. With that said, cryptocurrency staking can be a great way to earn some extra income, so long as you approach it with caution.

CHAPTER 5
PEER-TO-PEER LENDING

Peer-to-peer lending is a type of lending where people borrow and lend money to each other without going through a traditional financial institution. This can be done online through platforms that match lenders with borrowers.

Peer-to-peer lending can be a great way to earn passive income. You can typically earn higher interest rates than you would with a traditional savings account, and there is the potential to earn more if the borrower pays back their loan early.

One large benefit to this passive income stream is that it is significantly more "hands-off" than other passive income streams - there is a low level of literacy in the topic needed and instead, all you need to get started is access to an afore-mentioned lending platform and some funds that you are looking to lend out.

. . .

However, there are also some risks involved with peer-to-peer lending and these risks are usually at a much greater scale than other passive income streams. One big risk is that the borrower may simply not repay the loan, which could leave you out of pocket. There is also the risk that the platform you are using may not be reputable or may not have insurance in place to protect your investment.

Before you start investing in peer-to-peer lending, it's important to do your research and make sure you understand the risks involved. If done correctly, peer to peer lending can be a great way to earn passive income.

CHAPTER 6
CREATING A COURSE

f you know a particular skill very well, especially if it is a niche skill, one great passive income idea for you is to create an online course. This can be an online video course, an eBook, or even a physical product. Creating a course requires some upfront work, but once it's created, you can sell it over and over again and earn money each time someone buys it.

To get started, decide what type of course you want to create. It could be based on your own expertise or knowledge, or it could be something that you're passionate about. Once you know what your course will be about, start creating the content. This can include videos, tutorials, written lessons, and anything else that will help people learn what they need to know.

Once your course is created, you'll need to promote it and get people to buy it. You can do this through online marketing or by connecting with potential students through social media or other channels. If you sell your course for a one-time fee, you'll continue to earn money each time someone buys it. But if you want to create a recurring revenue stream, you can also sell access to your course on a monthly or yearly basis. This will give you a steady income that you can rely on month after month.

Creating a course is a great way to earn passive income. By putting in the upfront work, you can create something that will provide value to others and generate income for years to come. So, if you're looking for a way to turn some niche knowledge into a revenue stream while passing along some information, look into creating a course.

CHAPTER 7

PRINT-ON-DEMAND PRODUCTS

f you're looking for a way to create passive income, print-on-demand products are a great option. By creating designs and selling them as print-on-demand products, you can earn money without having to do any of the printing or shipping yourself.

Print-on-demand products can include things like t-shirts, mugs, tote bags, and more. To get started, you'll need to create some designs.

There are a few things to keep in mind when creating designs for print-on-demand products. First, your design should be eye-catching and unique. Second, it should be relevant to your target audience. And third, it should be easy to reproduce on a variety of different products.

You can create designs through a variety of different methods. If you are a more advanced designer, you can use professional level tools such as Adobe Illustrator. However, if you are a novice to graphic design, there is no need to fret! There are a plethora of design tools designed around giving creative novice's the ability to create professional-level designs using their own easy-to-use tools. An example of one of the most popular tools that does just that is Canva.

Once you have your designs ready, you can upload them to a print-on-demand site like Zazzle or Redbubble. Once your products are listed for sale, all you need to do is promote them! You can share them on social media, write blog posts about them, or even run ads through Google, Facebook (now Meta), or TikTok. When someone buys one of your products, the print-on-demand company will take care of the printing and shipping for you. All you have to do is sit back and collect your profits!

So, if you're looking for a way to make money while putting your creative-mind to work, consider creating print-on-demand products. With a little effort, you can start earning passive income from your designs in no time at all.

CHAPTER 8
ROBO-INVESTING

Robo-investing is a term used to describe the process of using technology to automatically invest in stocks or other assets. This can be done through online platforms or apps that provide recommendations or allow you to set up automatic investing plans. Some examples of these apps include Wealthfront, Betterment, and M1 Finance.

If you're interested in establishing passive income through robo-investing, there are a few things you should keep in mind. First, you'll need to decide which platform or app you want to use. There are a variety of options available, even more so than the few examples mentioned above. So, be sure to do your research before making a decision.

There are several advantages to using robo-investing to establish passive income. For one, it can help you save time by taking care of the research and investment decisions for you. Additionally, it can help you stay disciplined with your investing by following a pre-determined plan. And finally, it can help reduce your costs by eliminating the need for a human financial advisor.

Second, you'll need to establish an investment plan. This should include how much you're willing to invest and what types of investments you're interested in. Once you have a plan in place, the robo-investing platform will take care of the rest. A lot of robo-investing tools have automation in place that will help you stick to this plan and keep things as hands-off for you as possible.

Finally, remember that robo-investing is not a get-rich-quick scheme. Like any other type of investing, it carries risk - and based off of different options that you have selected in your robo-investing app, the risk can vary dramatically. However, if you're patient and disciplined, robo-investing can be a great way to build long-term passive income with very minimal input from you.

CHAPTER 9
DROPSHIPPING

Dropshipping is an e-commerce business model in which one can sell products online without having to carry any inventory. When a dropshipping store owner receives an order from a customer, they simply contact the supplier, who will then ship the products directly to the customer's doorsteps.

The most difficult aspect of dropshipping, and the one that can make or break your success, is finding the right product. Not all products are created equal and some will perform far better than others. So, how do you find the best dropshipping products?

The answer lies in understanding your niche and your target audience. Only by truly understanding these two areas can you hope to find products that they'll love and which will generate sales for your store. To be able to do this effectively, you need to immerse yourself in the world of your target audience, and this can be done a lot easier than it sounds.

. . .

Say, for example, you wish to start a dropshipping store with products in the skincare niche. For you to be able to do that, you can start following skincare YouTubers, TikTokers, and Instagram influencers, and see the types of products they recommend. You can then look deeper into those products and see the types of problems they solve. From there, you can find your own products that solve those same products, but as a fraction of the cost from other sources like eBay or AliExpress.

Once you have product selected, you can start to create an e-commerce storefront surrounding this idea. Websites like Shopify make it easy to create a beautiful, professional website with no prior web development experience. And once your store is up and running, you can start driving traffic to it through various marketing channels like Facebook Ads, Google Ads, Instagram influencer marketing, or even TikTok ads.

By following these steps, you can create a passive income stream through dropshipping that can provide you another revenue stream.

CHAPTER 10
SELLING STOCK PHOTOS AND VIDEOS

tock photos and videos are simply digital files that can be used by businesses and individuals for commercial purposes. For example, let's say you are a coffee shop owner who is creating their own website for their coffee shop. Now they want to add some photos to their website but hiring a photographer to come and take photos and videos of basic items, like a coffee pot pouring out coffee, would be very costly. So, this business owner could instead go to a stock video website and purchase a stock video matching the exact specifications that they need.

Creating stock photos and videos can be a lot easier as it sounds. All you really need is a bit of creativity and a quality camera - usually, the one built into your phone is of high-enough quality for most situations. You can think of any types of photos or videos that anyone might need. Like I mentioned in my previous example, a coffee shop might need a photo or video of coffee being poured out of a coffee pot. Conversely, a cleaning company might want a picture of a dirty kitchen. Really, the sky is the limit with ideas for stock photos and videos.

There are a number of stock photo and video websites where you can sell your content. Some of the most popular include Shutterstock, iStockphoto, and Getty Images.

When you sell your photos and videos on these websites, you'll earn a commission each time someone purchases your content. The commission rates vary depending on the website, but typically range from 20-40%.

If you're interested in earning passive income through selling stock photos and videos, then consider signing up for a free account on one of the many stock photo or video websites today. And start generating some extra cash flow!

CHAPTER 11
RENTING OUR SPACE ROOMS ON AIRBNB

Airbnb is a short-term rental platform that allows people to rent out their homes or rooms to guests. You can list your property on Airbnb for free, and set your own price and availability. With this platform, you can transform your unused space, like a spare bedroom or basement, into a money-making machine. Beyond listing just spare space in your home, you can also rent out your entire home when you are not there, such as when you are taking a vacation.

To get started, create an account on Airbnb and list your property. It pays to have professional-looking photographs in your listing to attract more attention from potential guests. Once your listing is approved, you can start welcoming guests! While there are no upfront costs to getting started on the platform, Airbnb takes a 3% commission on bookings.

The only other hands-on aspect to Airbnb is cleaning up after guests, and thankfully, this step can be easily outsourced. For a small fee, you can hire a professional cleaning service to come in and take care of everything after your guests have checked out. This way, you can earn passive income from your Airbnb rental without lifting a finger! The wonderful part of Airbnb is that you can also tack on a cleaning fee in your listing to help cover the cost of this.

If you have extra space in your home, consider renting out a room on Airbnb. This is a great way to earn some extra income, and it can even become passive income if you manage your listing well. Just be sure to follow all of the Airbnb rules and regulations, and take good care of your guests.

CHAPTER 12

CREATING A YOUTUBE CHANNEL

Now if you have a sociable personality and enjoy sharing your thoughts and ideas, starting a YouTube channel could be the perfect option for you. Not only is it a great way to make money passively (through ad revenue and other income streams), but it's also a fun and creative outlet that can help you connect with people all over the world.

Of course, before you can start earning any money from your YouTube channel, you need to put in some work to build up an audience and create videos that people will actually want to watch. There are many different topics that you can create videos about - be it, reviews about different products, providing commentary on other videos/news, or even just vlogging your day-to-day life. This part boils down to exactly what your passions are and what interesting aspects of your life others may also be interested in.

• • •

Once you start creating videos on YouTube, you can start to aim for the goal of attracting 1,000 subscribers and 4,000 hours of your content being watched in total because once you reach those thresholds, you can apply for the YouTube partner program which allows for YouTube to play ads on your videos and pay out ad revenue to you.

However, you can certainly earn revenue from YouTube before that using another method that we talked about previously in the book which if affiliate marketing. You can use your videos as a way to present different products to your viewers and direct them to use your affiliate links to purchase them so that you are able to earn commission off of those sales.

Overall, starting a YouTube channel is a great way to earn some passive income and can be a lot of fun if you choose a topic that you are passionate about!

CHAPTER 13
INVESTING IN REITS

I f you are interested in investing in real estate to earn passive income, but don't want to take on the headaches that go along with it, investing in a real estate investment trust might be the passive income idea for you! Real Estate Investment Trusts, or REITs, are investment vehicles that allow individuals to invest in large-scale real estate projects without having to go through the process of purchasing and managing property themselves.

REITs pool money from many investors and use it to purchase, develop, or finance income-producing real estate properties such as office buildings, shopping centers, apartments, warehouses, or hotels.

REITs must pay out at least 90% of their taxable income to shareholders in the form of dividends each year, which makes them an attractive option for investors who are looking for a steady stream of passive income.

.   .   .

There are two main types of REITs: Equity REITs and Mortgage REITs. Equity REITs own and operate income-producing real estate properties. They use the rental income from these properties to pay dividends to shareholders. Mortgage REITs, on the other hand, lend money to real estate developers, owners, and operators in the form of mortgages or loans. They use the interest payments on these loans to pay dividends to shareholders.

Some of the most popular REITs include Simon Property Group (SPG), Ventas, Inc. (VTR), and American Tower Corporation (AMT), and you can invest in these REITs on various stock exchanges using stock brokers.

Investing in REITs is a great way to diversify your portfolio and earn a steady stream of passive income. If you're interested in getting started, check out our guide to investing in REITs.

CHAPTER 14

RENT YOUR CAR OUT ON TURO

Turo is a car sharing marketplace that allows people to rent out their personal vehicles. As long as your vehicle is in good running condition and is eligible under the Turo vehicle criteria, you can list your vehicle on the site at no cost and allow others to rent it out when you are not using the vehicle.

Before you list your vehicle on Turo, the very first step you should take is to make sure that your vehicle is in sound mechanical and physical shape. This can mean taking your car to a mechanic for a checkup or getting the car detailed from a detailing shop.

Next, you'll need to take photos of your car and upload them to the site. Be sure to include clear, well-lit pictures of both the exterior and interior of your car. You'll also want to write up a description of your car, including its make, model, year, and any special features or amenities that it has. Ultimately, if you do these steps right, they are what will attract renters to your specific vehicle over others.

Once you've done all of this, you can then set a price for your car. Turo takes a 25% commission on all rentals, so be sure to factor that into your pricing. You'll also want to consider how much you think people will be willing to pay to rent your car.

Now once your car is listed on the site, Turo will take care of all the rental requests and bookings. Turo is able to go through the vetting process for renters and requires that they provide specific information to Turo such as their driver's license. Turo also provide insurance and 24/7 roadside assistance to renters, so you don't have to worry about those aspects when you are renting your vehicle our to renters.

If you're looking for a way to make some extra income while your car just sits in your parking spot, renting your car out on Turo is a great option.

CHAPTER 15
INVEST IN DIVIDEND STOCKS

ividend stocks, while lacking the glamor that other passive income ideas offer, are an excellent way to earn passive income. If you are unsure of what they are, dividend stocks are a type of stock (share in a company) that pays out regular "dividends" to shareholders. These dividends can be in the form of cash or shares of stock and are based upon various different factors like how the stock performed over the past quarter. Dividend stocks tend to be more stable than other types of stocks, making them an ideal choice for long-term investments. They can also offer investors a way to hedge against market volatility.

Getting started with investing in dividend stocks is a relatively straightforward process. The very first step that you want to take in this process is to actually select some different stocks that you would like to purchase. When choosing dividend stocks, it is important to consider things like the company's financial stability, dividend yield, and payout ratio. You should also take into account your own level of risk tolerance. While more risky stocks can captivate your attention with more media coverage and a higher potential to be profitable, we want to remember that our end goal is to not get stuck on the day-to-day volatile movements of stocks but instead, pick solid stocks that remain stable and offer a reliable dividend payout.

There are many different ways to invest in dividend stocks. The most common way to purchase dividend stocks is to register with a stock brokerage and then purchase the stock through them. This will allow you to actually hold the specific stock that you are looking to buy and while you continue to earn dividends the longer you hold the stock, you also have full control as to if you wish to sell that stock at a later time to recuperate your initial investment. You can also invest in them through mutual funds and exchange-traded funds (ETFs). These investment vehicles are slightly more complicated but still offer many benefits. With mutual funds, you are essentially pooling your money with other investors and then a professional fund manager will use that money to purchase a variety of different stocks on your behalf. This diversification can help to mitigate some of the risk associated with investing in dividend stocks. ETFs work in a similar way but tend to be more focused on specific sectors or indexes.

Overall, dividend stocks can provide investors with a great way to earn passive income and build long-term wealth with a relatively low barrier to entry and with low effort. However, with that said, they still require you to do a fair bit of research and risk your initial investment. But the one key benefit is that you are able to manage your own risk by deciding which stocks to buy and how many to purchase.

AFTERWORD

I hope this short book gave you some ideas about what might be possible for you, and that you will take the time to explore each of these opportunities in more detail. This is by no means the end-all-be-all of all the different passive income methods that exist. Passive income is a very broad discipline and my hope with this book was to just open your eyes to some of the potential that exists out there.

Passive income is a wonderful thing, and if you find a dependable stream of income that doesn't require much upkeep on your part, it can absolutely change your life. Passive income allows you to have more time and energy to do the things you love, while still making money. And, it's a great way to build long-term wealth to reach financial freedom. If you're looking for ways to make extra money, or even replace your current income, passive income is definitely something to consider!

So, what are you waiting for? Pick one of these ideas and get started. You'll be glad that you did and sooner than you think, you could have a nice little passive income stream going that requires very little upkeep from you! Isn't that the dream?